Hampstead Heath

The ACE project
'Literacy for Active Citizenship' series

Written by Dorothy Glynn
Photographs by Ayse Hassan

Hampstead Heath
© Learning Unlimited 2014

Published by Learning Unlimited Ltd as part of the Active
Citizenship and Literacy (ACE) project. The ACE project, led by
Learning Unlimited, was funded through the European Integration
Fund and delivered in partnership with Blackfriars Settlement,
Working Men's College and the Institute of Education.

Foreword

The ACE project
'Literacy for Active Citizenship' series

The Active Citizenship and English (ACE) project, led by Learning Unlimited and delivered in partnership with Blackfriars Settlement, Working Men's College and the Institute of Education, received funding from the European Integration Fund (July 2013 to June 2015).

The ACE project aimed to support non-EU women to develop their skills and confidence in English as well as the knowledge and confidence to take an active part in everyday life in the UK. As part of the project we wanted to produce a series of readers for our learners, and other adults also settling in the UK, which include stories about funny, personal and less typical aspects of everyday life in the UK. These books were written by learners and volunteers on the ACE project and the supporting activities have been developed by the Learning Unlimited team.

We hope you enjoy using the 'Literacy for Active Citizenship' series.

To find out more about the ACE project, please see:
www.learningunlimited.co/projects/ace

Hampstead Heath is a beautiful green
space. It is in North London.
It is very big.

There is a large pond.

Ducks and birds make their nests.

In the spring there are daffodils.

There is a swimming pool.

There is an athletics track.

There are tennis courts.

There are eight children's playgrounds.
There are cafes.

Visit Hampstead Heath, you will love it!

Key words

athletics track	a place where people can do sports like running or jumping
daffodils	yellow spring flowers
green space	somewhere with lots of grass and trees
nest	a place where a bird lays its eggs
pond	small lake, area of fresh water

Questions

1. Where is Hampstead Heath?

2. What can you see there?

3. What can you do there?

4. Have you ever been to Hampstead Heath? If so, what did you see? What did you think of it?

5. Do you live near a park? What can you see there? What can you do there?

6. Do you enjoy any sports? Which ones?

Activities

For downloadable activities, visit:
www.learningunlimited.co/resources/publications

Acknowledgements

Hampstead Heath was written by Dorothy Glynn and photographed by Ayse Hassan. We are grateful to them for being able to include their work as part of the 'Literacy for Active Citizenship' series.

To find out more about Learning Unlimited, its resources and published materials, CPD and teacher training programmes, project and consultancy work, please see: **www.learningunlimited.co**